T0273248

The Challenges
of China's Growth

THE HENRY WENDT LECTURE SERIES

The Henry Wendt Lecture is delivered annually at the American Enterprise Institute by a scholar who has made major contributions to our understanding of the modern phenomenon of globalization and its consequences for social welfare, government policy, and the expansion of liberal political institutions. The lecture series is part of AEI's Wendt Program in Global Political Economy, established through the generosity of the SmithKline Beecham pharmaceutical company (now GlaxoSmithKline) and Mr. Henry Wendt, former chairman and chief executive officer of SmithKline Beecham and trustee emeritus of AEI.

GROWTH AND INTERACTION IN THE WORLD ECONOMY:
THE ROOTS OF MODERNITY
Angus Maddison, 2001

IN DEFENSE OF EMPIRES
Deepak Lal, 2002

THE POLITICAL ECONOMY OF WORLD MASS MIGRATION:
COMPARING TWO GLOBAL CENTURIES
Jeffrey G. Williamson, 2004

GLOBAL POPULATION AGING AND ITS ECONOMIC CONSEQUENCES
Ronald Lee, 2005

THE CHALLENGES OF CHINA'S GROWTH
Dwight H. Perkins, 2006

The Challenges
of China's Growth

Dwight H. Perkins

The AEI Press

Publisher for the American Enterprise Institute
WASHINGTON, D.C.

Library of Congress Cataloging-in-Publication Data
Perkins, Dwight H. (Dwight Heald), 1934-

The challenges of China's growth / by Dwight H. Perkins.
     p. cm.
Includes bibliographical references.
  ISBN-13: 978-0-8447-7195-3 (pbk)
  ISBN-10: 0-8447-7195-3
  1. China—Economic conditions—2000- 2. China—Economic
policy—2000-.
  I. Title.

     HC427.95.P47 2006
     338.951—dc22

                                                          2006030828

     12 11 10 09 08 07   2 3 4 5 6

Contents

THE CHALLENGES OF CHINA'S GROWTH   1
    The Past Twenty-Seven Years   *3*
    Forecasting China's Future Economic Growth   *10*
    Sources of Political Tension   *26*
    The Impact of Future Economic Growth   *33*
    Implications for United States Policy   *41*

NOTES   45

REFERENCES   51

ABOUT THE AUTHOR   55

The Challenges of China's Growth
Dwight H. Perkins

For the past twenty-seven years China, according to official estimates, has enjoyed an average GDP growth rate of 9.4 percent per year.[1] GDP per capita in 2005 was eight times what it was in 1978. Some analysts argue that these official growth rates may overstate China's true rate of development, but there is also evidence that in some sectors they understate the true rate. No serious analyst, however, doubts that the pace of economic change has been rapid and that China has gone from being a very poor and economically weak nation in the 1970s to a still relatively low per capita income economy. It is now an aggregate economic force to be reckoned with on the world stage in 2006. If growth rates of this magnitude continue for another two decades to 2025, China will reach the level of per capita income of a South Korea today, but the overall size of the economy will be twenty-five times that of South Korea today and roughly equivalent to, or slightly larger than, the size of the U.S. economy in 2005. Abject poverty, using either the standard of $1 per day or $2 per day, will have been eliminated from this 20 percent of the world's population—a population that is twice the size of Europe and North America combined. Rising incomes have made China a major market for exporters of both natural resource products and high technology manufactures. For exporters of labor-intensive and some higher-end manufactures, however, China has become a formidable competitor. On the negative side, another economy the size of that of the United States' that, like the United States uses energy wastefully, will put a large strain on the world's environment. At the moment, China, in terms of energy use per unit of GDP, is even more wasteful than the United States. But China also is making vigorous efforts at present to raise the efficiency of its energy use. Where China will be in this regard two decades from now remains to be seen, but there is little doubt that China will be a major emitter of greenhouse gases and other pollutants by that time. China is also rapidly building up its military capacity, and that buildup is likely to continue as long as the economy keeps growing rapidly. But will this high growth rate of GDP continue and for how long?

Economies that grow rapidly for a time do not always continue along that path until they reach high income status. Argentina is the economy most often cited to illustrate this point. Argentina, in 1910, had a per capita income higher than that of Germany or France, but then growth slowed. From 1948 to 1959 and from 1974 through 1994 there was no growth whatsoever in Argentina's per capita income.[2] The misguided industrial policies of President Juan Peron and many of his successors, together with the 1980s debt crisis, account for the long periods of economic stagnation. But Argentina is one country among many. Between 1913 and 1950, despite two world wars and the Great Depression, average per capita income in eleven major West European countries did grow at a modest 1.4 percent per year, but in Germany per capita income in 1949 was virtually the same as in 1913. In France, it was not until 1949 that the per capita income climbed back to the level achieved in 1929.[3] In more recent times we have the example of the former centrally planned command economies of Eastern Europe and the former Soviet Union. There the transition to market economies came at the price of a deep depression for almost all of them. Ten years after the collapse of the Soviet-style economic system (in 1989) only Poland, the Czech Republic, Slovakia, and Hungary had recovered to or slightly surpassed the per capita income levels of the pre-1989 period.[4]

Thus there are many ways in which growth can be stopped. Prolonged warfare on one's territory is an obvious example. Misguided policies can achieve similar results. A decision to abandon one economic system for another can lead to years of adjustment before growth is restored. Nations heavily dependent on natural resources such as oil regularly go through cycles of boom followed by bust. But China has managed so far to avoid most of these pitfalls. China has enjoyed peaceful relations with its neighbors since at least 1980. China made the transition from a command economy to a market economy without a recession—to the contrary, growth accelerated immediately once the transition process began. And China is not a natural resource rich country that experiences boom and bust when mineral prices rise and fall. But China is also a country that has not made a transition to a political system that fosters active citizen participation in the political process. Can rapid economic growth in China continue without comparable changes in the political system? If changes in the political system are likely in the not-too-distant future, will those changes be gradual and peaceful or sudden and violent?

In the remainder of this essay, we will first review just how profound the economic and social changes of the past twenty-seven years have been. We will then turn to the question of whether the economic forces at work will allow this economic transformation to continue. As the brief discussion above makes clear, however, it is not economic forces that typically bring periods of sustained growth to a halt. The question for China is whether major disruptions in the domestic or international political arena are likely to change what in economic terms appears to be a very positive forecast. We will end with a few remarks about the implications of these likely trends for American policy toward China.

The Past Twenty-Seven Years

Before assessing the prospects for continued rapid growth in China, it is helpful to have a clearer picture of just what has, and has not, occurred in China over the past twenty-seven years in both economic and political terms. In 1974 and 1975, when I first visited the People's Republic of China, there was little construction going on in China's cities and construction cranes were simply not in evidence. New housing for urban residents was also not in evidence and nationwide even many engineers, professors, and medical doctors were squeezed into a tiny space where typically three people lived in an area of 13.2 square meters or 140 square feet that included the sleeping and living area[5], a tiny kitchen sometimes shared, and a shared bathroom. Farmers had roughly double that amount of space, but they often had to share it with their animals. By 2004, in contrast, China was building 479 million square meters of new urban residential space a year for an urban population of 543 million, and the average living space for an urban family of three had quintupled to 75 square meters or nearly 800 square feet.[6] If one looked out the window of a high-rise building in a city such as Shanghai, virtually every building one could see had been constructed within the past ten years.

Beginning in 1959 through 1961, because of Mao Zedong's Great Leap Forward and Rural Peoples Commune movements, over 30 million Chinese died prematurely, largely because of the indirect effects of inadequate levels of food. This was due partly to a decline in production and even more so to the poor distribution of the food supplies that did exist. Severe malnutrition came to an end with the recovery of agriculture after 1961, but rationing of grain and other key agricultural commodities continued through the 1970s. By the first years of the twenty-first century, however, food rationing was long gone and all but the poorest people in the more remote rural areas had enough to eat. The percentage of household income spent on food in the urban areas had fallen from 57 percent in 1981 to 38 percent in 2004, and the comparable Engel coefficient for the rural areas had fallen from 60 percent to 47 percent as incomes rose.

In the late 1970s and early 1980s there were no mobile phones and relatively few land line phones even in the urban areas. A call from Beijing to Shanghai could take hours to put through.[7] By 2004 there were 111 mobile phones per 100 households in urban China and there were 54.5 phones of all kinds per 100 households in the rural areas although there was considerable variation from one province to another. In 1981 hardly anyone in the rural areas had a television set (0.16 sets per 100 families), but by 2004 the great majority of rural residents had a television set and two-thirds of those sets were color.

Rural Chinese in 2004 still mainly rode bicycles, but one-third had motor bikes or used their hand tractors as mini-trucks (there were 19 mini-tractors per 100 households). In the cities passenger cars in the 1970s were reserved for high-level cadres and for important visitors. Production of motor vehicles other than trucks in 1981 was less than 70,000 per year, mainly of vehicles based on a Soviet design that was itself patterned on a U.S. design of the 1930s. In the first half of 2006, in contrast, passenger automobile production had reached 1.8 million vehicles, with Buick edging out Volkswagen for the top spot in terms of sales. In urban China in 2004, however, there were still only 2 automobiles per 100 households, a figure similar to that of Japan in the early 1960s.[8]

Even a small percentage of automobiles per capita in a country with a population of 1.3 billion, however, can create major traffic jams. Beijing has built one ring road after another and barely keeps up with the need. Nationwide in the 1970s, the main trunk highways linking major cities were typically two-lane paved roads, and truck traffic could be almost bumper to bumper for hundreds of miles on key roads. Feeder roads onto these main roads more often than not were unpaved. Beginning in the 1990s, however, Beijing decided it needed a modern countrywide highway system, and in the decade that followed, the nation constructed a multi-lane limited access highway system throughout the nation comparable to the American interstate system (although not quite as long as the latter because the main roads of the northwest and Tibet were still mostly two-lane and not particularly crowded with traffic).[9]

In the 1970s China's one airline used mainly old Soviet planes; purchase of its first ten Boeing 707s was a major event. By 2004 China had purchased 675 large and medium commercial aircraft from Boeing and Airbus, and its purchase of some smaller passenger planes was approaching 100 a year. Lufthansa, by way of comparison in 2006, had a fleet size (including subsidiary airlines) of 429 aircraft with 52 more on order.[10] American Airlines, the largest airline in the world, had 707 planes in 2005.[11] Virtually every provincial capital had a new modern airport with state-of-the-art navigation equipment. In 1979, by contrast, even a major city such as Wuhan had an airport that closed down, often for days, when there was a light rain.[12]

Most Chinese shared at least to some degree in this increased prosperity, but there are exceptions, mainly in the rural areas. In 1980 the average expenditure per capita in the rural areas (in 2004 prices) was just under 600 yuan and net income was 7 percent higher.[13] In 2004 net income (also in 2004 prices) was 2,936 yuan. Only 2.4 percent of rural households in 2004 had a per capita net income of 600 yuan or less. Another 10.1 percent had a household per capita income of less than 1,200 yuan. From personal observations made in designated poor counties in China's two poorest provinces (Gansu and Guizhou provinces in 1999), the poorest families in those villages were *very* poor indeed. Some slept under a thatched roof on slats a few feet above their privately owned hog that in turn resided next to the very crude kitchen. The children in these families were poorly clothed and barefoot and, despite compulsory education through eight grades, one saw young girls who were clearly not in school. But even in these designated poverty counties, however, the roads into them are often paved and many, and possibly most, have electricity. If they have a family member working in the factories on the coast, the children are well dressed and are clearly still in school. Their homes have tile roofs.

Converting these figures into U.S. dollars in order to compare China with the commonly used measures of poverty of $1 and $2 per day introduces some subjectivity, mainly because China has never officially calculated its GDP in purchasing power parity (PPP) dollars. According to World Bank estimates, the PPP exchange rate between the Chinese yuan and the U.S. dollar is 4.8 times the official dollar to yuan exchange rate.[14] Using the PPP exchange rate, therefore, the average net income of Chinese farmers in 1980 was $360, meaning that the average farmer just made the $1 per day poverty level. In 2004 the average PPP net income was $1,762 or well above the higher $2 per day poverty line. In 1980, over half of the rural population was below the $1 poverty line and much of the rest were below the $2 per day poverty line. According to Chen and Ravallion, the number of people in the entire Chinese population below the $1 per day poverty line in 2001 had fallen to 16.6 percent of the total population and the number below the $2 line in 2001 was 46.7 percent.[15] By 2005 these percentages would have fallen further. Whatever the validity of these precise numbers, there is no question that poverty in China has fallen dramatically over the past quarter century.

Economic progress in China over the past twenty-seven years, therefore, has been impressive. But the changes in China go well beyond income and infrastructure. China is less and less a nation of peasants, for example. The officially registered urban population has risen from 17.9 percent of the total to 41.8 percent. Total employment in the primary sector (which is mostly agriculture) fell from 70.5 percent in 1978 to 46.9 percent.[16] Along with this shift out of agriculture have come a number of changes, not all of which have had a positive impact on welfare. The rural health system built up under the communes has fallen apart under free markets, and few rural people have any health insurance. Moving to the cities does not help, because few migrants from the rural areas can afford the cost of urban health care. The household registration system also makes it difficult for rural migrants to put their children in urban schools. We shall explore these problems at greater length below.

Perhaps least appreciated by the world outside of China are the major changes that have already taken place in the political sphere and in the populations' access to information. While Mao Zedong was still alive and his wife Jiang Qing dominated the culture world, even the Chinese elite had very limited access to information about what was happening in the outside world or to what was happening in China itself. The main publication available to a narrow elite was *cankao xiaoxi* (reference news) that had clippings from the Western press among other sources. The open press did little more than publish official decrees of the government and reports on important visitors from abroad. Even popular entertainment, such as Beijing operas, was limited by the cultural czars to a handful of performances that gave the "correct" political message. People were afraid to talk frankly about issues with their neighbors and even close friends for fear that they would then be dragged in front of a meeting to confess and self-criticize their behavior—or worse. Suicide not uncommonly followed on the worst of these confrontations.

Contact with foreigners was even more dangerous. Simply having a relative living abroad could be grounds for persecution. Chinese speaking to foreigners made sure that the contact was officially sanctioned and that they were always together with another Chinese who could testify to what they had said to the foreigner. One member of what was then called the U.S. Liaison Office in Beijing found he could only talk to individual Chinese without these strictures if he happened to be riding alongside them on his bicycle and the Chinese citizen involved knew he could always veer off quickly and be gone if he saw he was being observed by someone who might report him. When contact with foreigners was authorized, the conversations seldom veered from officially sanctioned positions on all issues except at the very highest levels. At banquets, the one safe topic was the food.[17] By any reasonable standard, China prior to 1976 was a totalitarian state in the full sense of that term. Using the Friedrich-Brzezinksi definition of totalitarianism China was a totalitarian nation par excellence. In particular, China during the first three decades of Communist Party rule was a state that had an official all-encompassing ideology to which "general adherence was demanded." The Chinese people were not allowed to passively adhere to this ideology; they had to actively support it in numerous study (xuexi) meetings and more public forums. The demand for adherence was backed up not only by police terror but also by a pervasive community mutual surveillance system.[18]

Fast forward to the twenty-first century and the situation could not be more different. Millions of Chinese have traveled abroad singly and in groups. Hundreds of thousands have studied at, or been visiting scholars to, universities in North America, Europe, and Japan. One-on-one conversations between Chinese and foreigners are common and most of the time no one representing the security apparatus is trying to listen in (although there are, of course, exceptions). The foreign press is subjected to considerable surveillance by the authorities, but most other foreigners are ignored unless they are involved in particularly sensitive issues.

The number of Chinese with access to the Internet has passed 100 million and is increasing rapidly. Some sites on the Internet are blocked, but the vast majority are not. And even for the blocked sites, there is reason to believe that those who want to get through to the banned sites often can do so.[19] Western books, magazines, and newspapers are available to most who have the money to pay for them, although there is still censorship. There are dozens of television channels available showing thousands of movies, documentaries, news, and a wide variety of entertainment. Whatever one thinks of the quality of what is shown on television, there is a great deal of it.

The main area where there has been very limited change is in the nature of the political system that governs China. The Chinese Communist Party has a complete monopoly on all major government positions and policy decisions. The top leadership of the party is formally selected by the party Central Committee but in practice it is picked by a small group of Politburo members. There are more candidates for membership on the Central Committee than there are positions, so disfavored candidates can be, and are, kept off the Committee, but the number so affected is very small. The party has also broadened the criteria for those allowed to be party members to include private business people. In effect the Chinese Communist Party has abandoned its belief in maintaining a government monopoly over the economy, a central tenet of the ideology with which it governed China until very recently.

Elections involving the population at large exist mainly at the village level. At that level there is often real competition for slots to lead the locality, and officials who are incompetent or worse are often defeated. China's experiment with village democracy, however, at present appears to be mainly directed at curbing local cadre abuses and is not necessarily a model that will be gradually expanded to include higher level political units and the cities.

Corruption among officials in China is widespread. The Transparency International Index places China tied for No. 78 out of a total of 159 countries ranked with a raw score of 3.2 (with 10 being no corruption and 1 being completely corrupt). The Chinese-majority societies of Singapore and Hong Kong by comparison were ranked

Nos. 5 and 15 with raw scores of 9.4 and 8.3.[20] The raw index score in this index may be a better indicator than China's ranking against other countries. China, for example, is only 1.1 higher than countries in the bottom 10 percent of all those rated but is 3.0 below No. 30 on the list and 6.2 below Singapore. Put differently, China is grouped with a large number of very corrupt nations even if it is near the top of the list of the very corrupt. The country has a long way to go to reach a level comparable to that of countries that most outside observers would consider only mildly corrupt (Italy and South Korea at 5.0 for example).

Rather than rely on elections that could "throw the rascals out," China has mainly attacked the problem with severe criminal penalties—including death for the worst cases. China could also ease the corruption problem by ridding itself of the myriad of licenses and permits needed to do business that have caused China to be ranked 91st out of 155 ranked countries in the World Bank's ranking of the "ease of doing business."[21] When it comes to obtaining licenses, for example, out of 155 countries, China ranks No. 146 in terms of the number of procedures necessary, with 30 procedures that take 363 days to complete, and is tied for No. 148 in terms of the time required to secure them. Raising China's ranking in these areas—mainly by eliminating licenses and similar procedures—would do more to curtail corruption than any realistic number of executions.

Can China sustain this seeming contradiction between having a dynamic economy and an increasingly open society on the one hand and a political system that is slow to change and is widely perceived as being very corrupt on the other? Before trying to answer that question, however, we must first explore whether China's economy will continue on its high growth trajectory.

Forecasting China's Future Economic Growth

Forecasting China's long-term growth prospects is a very different exercise from forecasting whether China will grow rapidly next year or will face a hard landing and a recession because of the excessively high growth rate of 2006. All kinds of external shocks and short-term policy mistakes can affect growth from year to year. Since the reform period began, China's annual GDP growth rate has fluctuated between a low of 4.2 percent (in 1989 and 1990) and a high of 14.1 percent (in 1993). Forecasting the extent of growth over a decade or longer generally must take into account these short-term influences. To forecast China's long-term economic growth prospects, one needs to begin with an understanding of how the high long-term growth of the past twenty-seven years was achieved. The methodology best suited to answer that question is growth accounting or sources of growth analysis mainly from the supply side.

Following Robert Solow, we use the production function:

$$Y = f(K, L, t)$$

where Y is GDP, K is the stock of capital, L is the labor force, and t is the shift in productivity over time. This equation (with certain assumptions), can be differentiated and rearranged into the following form:

$$g_y = w_k \times g_k + w_l \times g_l + a$$

where g_y is the growth rate of GDP, g_k is the growth rate of the capital stock, g_l is the growth rate of the employed labor force (and in the quality of that labor force as measured by its education level), w_k and w_l are the shares in national income of the income of capital and labor respectively, and a is the rate of growth of productivity—usually referred to as total factor productivity (TFP). The growth accounting data for China from 1952 through 2005 are presented in table 1 on the following page.

The central point of this table is that the major difference between China's slow economic growth prior to 1979 and its rapid growth from that year onward is driven mostly by the shift from negative total factor productivity growth in the 1957–1978 period to strongly positive total factor productivity averaging 3.8 percent per year from

TABLE 1

SOURCES OF CHINA'S ECONOMIC GROWTH

Period		Growth Rate				Shares of Contribution to GDP growth	
	GDP	Capital Stock	Labor and Human Capital	TFP*	Capital	Labor and Human K	TFP*
1952–2005	6.95	8.28	2.66	1.9	51.2	21.8	27.1
1952–57	6.52	6.80	1.71	2.6	44.9	15.0	40.1
1957–65	2.41	6.18	2.11	−1.5	110.4	50.0	−60.3
1965–78	4.87	7.72	3.15	−0.3	68.2	36.9	−5.2
1978–2005	9.46	9.45	2.75	3.8	43.0	16.6	40.4
1978–85	9.73	7.97	4.56	3.7	35.2	26.7	38.1
1985–90	7.70	9.26	2.91	2.1	51.7	21.6	26.7
1990–95	11.73	9.33	2.20	6.3	35.7	10.7	53.6
1995–2000	8.58	8.52	1.61	4.0	42.7	10.7	46.6
2000–05	9.48	12.42	1.81	3.1	56.3	10.9	32.8

SOURCES AND METHODOLOGY: See Perkins and Rawski, 2006, appendix.
NOTE: TFP = Total Factor Productivity.

1979 onward. Formally, the growth rate of the capital stock after 1978 accounts for slightly more of the growth than productivity (43 percent versus 40.4 percent), but this is misleading. The reforms that began in late 1978 did not raise the rate of capital formation as a share of GDP. The rate of investment as a share of GDP changed little from the pre- to the post-1978 period. Reforms that caused the jump in productivity by raising the rate of GDP growth thus also raised the rate of growth of capital (since the same share of investment was now applied to a higher level of GDP).

High productivity growth probably also had something to do with why the rate of investment as a share of GDP remained so high after 1978. Before the reform period, the rate of investment was driven by the government's decision to generate a high savings rate mainly through creating high monopoly profits in industry that were then taxed away from the enterprises and subsequently returned in the form of state-led investment. The rate of investment in this earlier period was thus an administrative decision made by the government and was not driven by the rate of return on that investment. After 1978, and particularly by the 1990s and during the first years of the twenty-first century, however, investment was increasingly in private profit–oriented hands and high productivity produced high profits that led to high rates of investment.

Sustaining high GDP growth rates in China over the next two decades, therefore, is first and foremost a question of continuing to generate high growth in total factor productivity. Forecasting productivity growth, however, is a highly subjective exercise, so we will begin with the somewhat easier part of the story—forecasting the contribution to GDP growth of capital formation and the growth of the labor force and the quality of that labor force (human capital).

In a closed economy without access to foreign capital, the rate of investment is driven in part by the rate of return to that investment but also by the level of domestic savings that can be mobilized to finance that investment. China today is no longer a closed economy in that sense since foreign direct investment has reached $60 billion a year in 2004 and 2005. However, as large as that figure is, it is less than 10 percent of total Chinese investment that, as of 2004, was an extraordinary 44.2 percent of GDP—which translates in U.S. dollar terms into more than $700 billion at the official exchange rate. Thus, the rate of investment in China still depends to an important degree on whether China's current, very high savings rate remains high in the future.

A nation's savings rate is the product of savings decisions by several distinct groups—those of individual households, of the government, and of industrial and commercial enterprises. Future government savings is likely to be low due primarily to its large unfunded pension liabilities, the fact that commercial banks still require refinancing of an excessive number of nonperforming assets, and because the social welfare system in general, and the health care system in particular, will require large-scale government support. If high growth continues, however, enterprise profits are likely to remain high, and a substantial portion of those profits will be plowed back into investment. At present, enterprise profits tend to be concentrated in the energy sector, but that could change over time.

The most important source of savings in China today, however, is households, and households save for a number of reasons. Many, for example, save in order to accumulate funds to purchase large consumer durables. The privatization of housing has created another reason to save now that families must purchase their homes. Expanding consumer credit and larger and longer term mortgages could erode these reasons for saving over time. If, as argued below, China must shift aggregate demand from a dependence on rapid export growth to domestic consumption and investment, then an expanded consumer lending program would be a way of accomplishing this shift.

The major motive for saving in households around the world, however, is to prepare for retirement. The model that best captures this effect is the life-cycle model of savings that relates the level of household savings to a country's dependency ratio: the ratio of children and the elderly who are not in the labor force, to those who are in the labor force. The dependency ratio from 1990 to 2025 is presented in table 2.

The central point in this table is that China's dependency ratio has been low for some time and is likely to remain low for the next two decades. The reason for this low dependency ratio is due partly to the one-child family policy that began in the 1970s. All new entrants to the labor force over the past decade and a half and over the coming decade and a half are a product of the one-child policy. Only a sharp increase in the birth rate during the next five years would change that picture, and then only for the years 2021 to 2025, when those born today and in the next few years turn fifteen years of age (and even those are likely still to be in the education system longer than is the case today).

China's workforce today, in contrast, was mostly born after 1952 through the early 1970s when Mao Zedong and other Chinese leaders thought that the bigger the Chinese population the better. Those born in 1952 are not yet of retirement age, even using the early retirement age applied to the state sector. With most adults in good health staying actively occupied until their mid-60s, retirement of China's

TABLE 2
CHINA'S DEPENDENCY RATIO, 1990–2025

	Total Population (in millions)	Population Aged 16–65 (in millions)	Ratio Age 16–65 to total	Dependency Ratio
1990	1,143	737	0.64	0.36
2000	1,267	853	0.67	0.33
2005	1,306	909	0.7	0.3
2015	1,387	991	0.715	0.285
2025	1,472	968	0.66	0.34

SOURCES AND METHODOLOGY: See Perkins and Rawski, 2006.

"baby boom" generation will not really begin until after 2015. In table 2, there is in fact a slight rise in the dependency ratio between 2015 and 2025, but only back to the levels of the 1990s. After 2025, the picture begins to change dramatically. Most of the "baby boomers" will be retired by 2035 (the youngest will be sixty-three years of age) and, with increasing life expectancy in China, more and more of them will be living into their eighties and beyond. The workforce, in contrast, will be made up entirely of products of the one-child policy. China's dependency ratio will soar and the household savings rate will no doubt fall, but that is beyond the period with which we are concerned in this essay. For the next two decades, the savings rate is likely to remain high and, if the investment opportunities are there, the investment rate will keep up with the savings rate. Capital formation in China will continue at a rapid pace.

China's labor force, however, will not continue to grow at the past rate. As those born in the 1950s begin to retire and are replaced by the one-child policy generation, the numbers of people in the labor force will stagnate and may even decline slightly. Currently 70 percent[22] of those of school age (aged six to twenty-one) are now in school, and that percentage will rise, perhaps to 75 to 80 percent, as China moves toward universal high school education and increasing university enrollments. The reduction in the labor force, because of increased time in school, will probably be offset by simultaneous increases in the age of the older-age groups still in the workforce (particularly if the pension systems remain as weak as they are today). In terms of growth accounting, the increase in education will mean that the quality of the labor force is steadily rising, and this will mean that labor will continue to make a positive contribution to growth—but a very modest one.

This analysis of the contribution of the labor force and human capital to growth, however, leaves out one important element that, in the above calculations, shows up as total factor productivity, but is in reality a contribution to growth by labor. In China in 2004, there were still 352.7 million workers in the primary sector, and most were farmers cultivating less than 122 million hectares of arable land.[23] The United States, in contrast, cultivates more than 110 million hectares of land with only 3 million farmers. Over the next two decades, a large share of China's farm workers will leave farming and move to jobs in industry and services, with most of those jobs being in China's cities. Based on the differential in urban and rural wages of unskilled workers of roughly three to one,[24] the migration of farm workers to the cities should approximately triple the productivity of those workers. If employment in industry and services rises by 10 million jobs a year over the coming two decades, migrants from the countryside will be the ones filling those jobs.[25] The result will be the migration of 200 million farmers out of agriculture into the cities over the next two decades. We will explore the broader implications of this massive migration further below.

Migration from the countryside to the cities, rising education levels of the workforce in general, and a continued high rate of investment should keep China's GDP growing for at least the next two decades, but, in the absence of a high level of total factor productivity (TFP) growth, China's GDP growth will be in the 3 to 5 percent range. As the data in table 1 indicate, TFP growth during the past twenty-seven years of the reform period averaged 3.8 percent a year. This high TFP growth, however, was generated by a series of reforms that corrected some of the major distortions that hurt productivity growth during the command economy period between 1955 and 1978. In the 1979–1981 period, for example, China abolished the rural commune system of collective farming and went back to household agriculture. The result was a large jump in farm output between 1978 and 1984, but it was a one-shot jump. Agricultural value-added growth rates reverted part of the way back to the long-term trend rates of the pre-1978 period after 1984.[26]

The other major change in the first years of the reform period was the opening up of the economy to foreign trade. The rapid expansion of exports made possible the rapid expansion of inputs of key materials and equipment that certainly contributed in a major way to productivity growth and continues to do so to this day. But the gap between imported and domestically produced technology is not as great today as it was in those early years.

Beginning in 1984, China also experienced an explosion in industrial productivity when it freed up most industrial inputs to be sold on the market rather than allocated by administrative means in accordance with the central plans. The main beneficiaries were the township and village enterprises (TVEs) that were owned or controlled by localities. Unlike large state-owned enterprises, the TVEs responded to market forces because that was the main way to make money. The TVEs also faced hard budget constraints because the local governments lacked the resources to bail them out if they experienced losses—again unlike the large state firms that could go back to the banks for loans that they might or might not pay back. Prior to the 1984 reforms, however, TVEs had to apply to the central planners for administrative allocation of key inputs, an application process where they received a low priority. With the reforms, they could purchase what they needed, albeit at higher prices than the previous state-set prices. The TVE boom that ensued lasted into the mid-1990s and was the main force sustaining the high rate of industrial growth in that period. But by the late 1990s, the TVE boom had also lost much of its momentum.

Finally, it was in the late 1990s that foreign direct investment (FDI) in China took off. In 1990 and in the years immediately preceding, FDI averaged between $3 and $4 billion per year, but by 1995 that figure had jumped to $37.5 billion, and in 2004 it passed $60 billion for the first time. The money itself was not so important, since China had large alternative sources of foreign exchange (mainly export earnings that reached $149 billion in 1995, $224 billion in the year 2000, and $762 billion in 2005). What did matter for productivity growth were the technology, the management expertise, the quality control, and the access to foreign markets that accompanied the foreign direct investment. It is likely that FDI accounts for a large share of the 3.1 percent annual TFP growth in the first six years of the twenty-first century (see table 1). But it is also likely that the sharp increase in FDI since the early 1990s will not continue long into the future. FDI into China appears to be leveling off at the current high levels, and annual realized FDI has only increased on average by 3.7 percent per year since 1997. Thus, continuously rising FDI is not likely to be a major source of TFP growth, although continued high levels of FDI will no doubt contribute to future TFP growth.

What then will support high TFP growth in the future if many of the past sources appear to have run out of steam? One source is likely to be the continued privatization of much of the modern sector of the Chinese economy. China has never had a formal privatization program, and, in fact, the word privatization is not used by the government to describe what is going on in industry and services. Furthermore, it is not easy to precisely estimate the size of the private sector in China, because ownership classifications keep changing. Between 1999 and 2002, for example, the state-owned enterprise share of industrial output in firms with sales above 5 million yuan fell from 30.56 percent to 15.59 percent. But most of this drop occurred because state-owned enterprises in large numbers were listing on the Shanghai and Shenzhen stock exchanges and were reclassified as shareholding enterprises. The share of state-owned industrial enterprises and state-controlled shareholding enterprises also declined, but only from 48.92 percent to 40.78 percent.[27] Outside of agriculture, the one area that is largely and unambiguously privatized is urban housing. Housing that was typically owned by the state industrial enterprises was sold usually at bargain prices to the occupants and most new housing is being bought by individual families.

Most of the shareholding, former state-owned enterprises, however, still operate much like they did in the recent past when they
were formally state owned. The government and the Communist
Party still have the major say in selection of management, and the
government in fact still has majority control of the shares in most of
these enterprises. There are a few "independent" directors on the
boards, but there is little evidence that these independent directors
have much influence. If shareholding is to really involve more than
just a vehicle for raising capital and is to truly transform state-owned
enterprises into modern market- and profit-oriented corporations,
the government and the party will have to become minority shareholders at the most and will have to allow boards of directors elected
by the majority shareholders to select top management. The Chinese
Communist Party has surrendered direct power over the economy
in other sensitive areas, notably in agriculture, so there is no reason
to doubt that they won't do so in this area as well, but they had made
little progress in this regard by 2006.

The TVEs are proceeding much more rapidly toward true privatization. In the late 1980s and early 1990s, most were classified as
collectives since that was a politically more acceptable term and it
reflected the fact that the local community, mainly through local
governments, had a major role in the operation of these local enterprises. Local governments still have a major role in these enterprises,
but management is increasingly in the hands of a private owner. In
the current climate that is friendlier to outright private ownership,
TVEs apparently no longer feel a need for the kind of political protection provided by being collectively owned.[28]

Goods and services in China have been distributed mostly
through market mechanisms since the middle to late 1990s. The
dual price system set up in the mid-1980s, where goods were partly
distributed through markets and partly through government administrative channels, died a natural death.[29] Firms with goods to sell
preferred to offer them on the market, where prices were higher, and
they used various methods to avoid use of the administrative channels. Firms purchasing goods knew that, if they wanted their key
inputs on time, they were more likely to get them through the mar-

ket than from the planners. The government, which introduced the dual price system mainly to appease powerful state enterprises that did not want to pay higher prices, had little incentive to stop the steady erosion of the quantity of goods allocated through administrative channels.

Markets for factors of production—labor, land, and capital—are less well developed than in the case of goods and services. There is a fairly well developed urban land market, although it is plagued with political influence and other distortions. There is no regular market for rural land, however, and there are inefficiencies created by farmers who leave their land for the city but use various methods to hold onto their rights to the land. In such cases, the land is often underutilized, and incentives to invest in the land are weak. In other parts of the country, the local authorities periodically redistribute the land under their jurisdiction to reflect changes in the demographic makeup of their localities. These interventions do sometimes serve equity considerations, and so moving toward greater efficiency by letting the market handle rural land transactions may not be politically acceptable. Corrupt land deals in the rural areas, whether they make more efficient use of the land or not, are a major source of political tension and violence. Typically these land deals involve local officials pushing farmers off their land to make way for a factory or other commercial use.[30]

The main inefficiency in the urban labor market is the differential treatment of officially registered urban residents versus new migrants from the rural areas who are still registered as rural residents. We will discuss this issue further below. Government-directed administrative allocation of labor, the primary method of skilled labor allocation prior to the reform period, has largely disappeared.

In terms of the impact on economic growth, however, the largest negative influence at present arises from the underdeveloped and politically distorted nature of China's capital markets. Like most developing countries, China's capital markets are underdeveloped. The main financial institutions are the commercial banks, and these banks since early on in the reform period have lent mainly to the less efficient state enterprises.[31] Because the state enterprises were used to having their investment needs met through the government budget, they often treated bank loans as virtual grants and made no effort to pay them back. The result, as is now well known, was a massive buildup of nonperforming loans in the banking system.[32]

China has been struggling with how to clean up the balance sheets of the commercial banks and is doing so with some success. Nonperforming assets officially have fallen from 35 percent in 1999[33] to around 8 percent in 2005. The true figures are widely believed to be higher than these official estimates, but there is no doubt that the share of nonperforming loans has declined, although even officially it is still at a high level. Equally serious from an efficiency point of view, the banks continue to direct a large portion of their loans to the state-owned or state-controlled sector because loans to the state sector are seen as politically safe even if they often aren't commercially safe. The more dynamic private sector (other than enterprises with large amounts of foreign direct investment) has difficulty getting access to capital. This situation is beginning to change, but slowly.

The Shanghai and Shenzhen stock exchanges are similar to the banks in that they mainly serve the capital needs of the state sector. Firms allowed to list on these exchanges are overwhelmingly state-owned enterprises or state-controlled shareholding enterprises. Other financial institutions, notably the insurance companies, are still in the early stages of development and are not yet major players on the Chinese capital markets. Thus, China's financial system has a long way to go to be the kind of efficient system that can sustain economic growth. From a forecasting point of view, that situation can be seen as either an advantage for the future or a disadvantage. It is a disadvantage if China fails to fundamentally reform and develop its financial institutions, particularly the commercial banks, up to international standards. In that case, the inability of dynamic non-state firms to access capital could be seriously hampered and China could even end up in a situation similar to that in Japan during its fourteen years of economic stagnation (1991–2004). Japan's stagnation was to a significant degree the result of a banking system loaded down with nonperforming assets that was reluctant to lend to anyone other than the government and already established firms such as Toyota.

The weak state of China's financial system, however, also can be seen as an advantage for future productivity growth. If China continues to take forceful steps to strengthen its financial system and put it in the service of the whole economy, not just the favored state sector, China could achieve large efficiency gains. Our own estimate is that reforms in the financial system will continue at a steady pace and will be aided by China's commitments under the WTO to open its financial sector to full foreign participation and competition. China has done well to date with a very weak financial system. It should do better as it gradually weeds political considerations out of its financial decision making.

In a full market economy, it is not just the allocation of goods and services or allocation of factors of production that is handled through decentralized decisions of the enterprises themselves. The basic direction of industrial development, other than in the defense industry, is largely left to market forces. Issues such as bankruptcy and mergers or acquisitions are also handled by the parties directly involved—the creditors and debtors in the case of bankruptcy, and the firms acquiring or being acquired in the case of mergers and acquisitions. These transactions are subject to rules laid down by the legislature, but enforcement of those rules is left to independent judges. In much of East and Southeast Asia, in contrast, it is the executive branch of the government that takes the lead in these areas.

The most influential model for state-led growth in Asia was that developed by the Ministry of International Trade and Industry (MITI) in Japan and altered to fit the somewhat different conditions of South Korea, particularly during the reign of President Park Chung Hee in the 1960s and 1970s. The executive branch of the government did not try to comprehensively plan industrial development. Instead it attempted to determine which industries would be critical to the next stage of development and then actively promoted those industries through directed bank loans (the government either owned the banks outright or had enormous influence over bank lending decisions). The executive branch also provided access to foreign exchange and critical imports (in the early stages of development when foreign exchange was scarce and was tightly controlled). Implementation was actually carried out by private firms for the most part, but these were private firms willing to do the bidding of the government.

In this kind of industrial policy, if an enterprise failed because it faithfully carried out the wishes of the government planners, the government was obligated to help the firm get out of difficulty (by forgiving past loans or by lending more funds to tide the firm over, for example). If the firm failed because of its own shortcomings, the government still might intervene to save the firm but might replace the existing management. If the government felt that a different industrial structure was appropriate, it could pressure firms to merge with others or get out of particular lines of business in order to reduce "excessive" competition. This pressure did not always have the desired effect (MITI's failed attempt to force consolidation in the Japanese automobile industry is one of the best known examples), but, more often than not, the private firms tried to implement what the government desired. In South Korea after the financial crisis of 1997–1998, the government used its control over the banking system (itself largely bankrupt) to force some firms into liquidation (Daewoo) and to pressure others to give up some components in order to concentrate on what the government felt the particular firm did best.

China, more or less by default, has inherited this kind of an industrial policy, but has tried to implement such a policy under conditions very different from those that prevailed in Japan and South Korea. When China abandoned comprehensive central planning, it did not move toward a system of laissez-faire markets patterned on those of, say, Hong Kong. Instead, China retained an active interest in promoting particular industries, notably automobiles, and thus the MITI-Korean approach has had great appeal. China also had to deal with thousands of enterprises that began to experience financial losses once prices for their products had to be adjusted to reflect competitive market forces as opposed to the prior system of government-set monopoly prices. In addition, enterprises under comprehensive planning were typically single factories that were little more than subordinate offices of giant industrial ministries. When these enterprises were made into truly independent firms, China ended up with one of the least concentrated industrial organizations anywhere in the world. Consolidation of this fragmented industrial organization structure was clearly desirable, but how was this consolidation to be accomplished?

Thus, China's government by the 1990s faced all kinds of decisions about the future path of industry, and the question was what to do about it. The full market approach would have been to leave these issues to be dealt with by the individual enterprises in response to market forces. But China was not in a position to do that because institutions critical to allowing markets to make these decisions efficiently did not exist. Specifically, China's judicial system was extremely weak and completely incapable of handling complex issues such as bankruptcies and mergers. China's courts weren't terribly effective at resolving even simpler commercial disputes. Judges were not well trained, and they certainly were not independent of the executive branch of the government. After decades during which the judicial system was neglected or abandoned (Mao at one point abolished the legal profession), judges had limited authority and their decisions could be overruled—or simply ignored—and not just by high government officials.

Consequently the Chinese government had to have an activist industrial policy, but it lacked an essential ingredient possessed by those implementing industrial policy in Japan and South Korea. In Japan and South Korea, industrial policy was carried out by technocrats, and decisions were made mainly on technical grounds and not for political or for rent-seeking purposes (corruption). Corruption and politics certainly existed in these two countries but they played a minimum role in industrial policy, at least in the early stages of their development (the 1950s and 1960s in Japan and the 1960s and 1970s in South Korea).[34] In China, it is hard to imagine a major industrial policy decision that would not be influenced by politics and/or rent-seeking. China's ranking in the Transparency

International Index discussed above makes it clear that corruption is pervasive in Chinese decision making. Technocrats do play some role in Chinese industrial policy decisions, but almost never do they have the primary or final say on major issues. Furthermore, China's very size makes an activist industrial policy emanating from Beijing difficult. South Korea's Park Chung Hee could meet with the leaders of all of the major industries and firms once a month and could listen to their concerns and try to solve the problems they were having with the government. It is difficult to imagine anything comparable being attempted by President Hu Jintao or Premier Wen Jiabao. There were 219,000 industrial enterprises above a certain minimum size (in 2004), and they were scattered across the country.[35]

Again returning to the issue of forecasting China's future productivity growth, China's current situation with regard to industrial policy can be seen in both a positive and a negative light. On the negative side, China clearly has no choice for the immediate future other than to pursue an activist industrial policy with a good deal of government intervention, however inefficient that intervention might be. The institutions needed to avoid this outcome, notably the legal and regulatory system, are simply too weak to take many tasks over from the executive branch of the government. On the positive side, if China does set out to build the necessary legal and regulatory institutions and moves steadily away from an activist MITI-style industrial policy, the results are likely to be a big boost in productivity.

Will China take this path? There is no question that China is gradually trying to strengthen its legal institutions, and more and more people are going to the courts in an attempt to resolve disputes. On the other hand, the Chinese government is still full, in its upper ranks, of former planners who see an active role for themselves and for the government. While there is little doubt that China has the potential to make major improvements in the supporting institutions of a full market economy, it is much less clear whether the Chinese leadership sees activist intervention in industrial policy in a negative light. If it persists with the system as it exists today, growth over the long run could suffer.

Sources of Political Tension

Failure to continue to vigorously push reform of the supporting institutions of a full market economy, therefore, could slow economic growth significantly, but no plausible pace of economic reform is likely to bring growth to a halt or even to bring growth to a level of less than 5 percent a year. Social tensions and the political changes that could result, in contrast, could have a larger impact and could even bring growth to a halt. We do not think that this no-growth scenario is likely, but the social tensions in China today are real enough and could lead to fundamental political changes that could interrupt growth, at least for a time.

The tensions that are getting the most coverage in the Western press are largely connected with misappropriation of land by corrupt local officials. These land deals gone bad appear to be a major source of the rising number of officially reported incidents that have involved some form of higher level police and government intervention. Basically, given the weakness of the courts, local people, particularly in the rural areas, sometimes make known their complaints with authority by resorting to demonstrations and violence. The long-term solution to this problem is to define rural property rights clearly, strengthen the courts so that they can be a fair and efficient way of resolving property rights disputes, and strengthen local cadre elections so that more of the corrupt local officials are weeded out. Accomplishing these changes will be a formidable task, but at least it is reasonably clear what needs to be done.

Other sources of potential and actual social tension in China do not have such straightforward "solutions." At the most general level, rapid economic development, wherever it occurs, eases some sources of social and political tension and exacerbates others. High rates of growth, for example, are usually accompanied by rapidly rising wages and household incomes, and that usually contributes to political stability. This has been the case in China. Large portions of the urban population in China, in particular the younger cohorts who are best positioned to take advantage of the many new economic opportunities, are busy getting rich and don't have the time or the inclination to participate in political protests. On the other hand, rapid economic growth also means rapid structural change in both the economy and the society, and structural change inevitably leaves many people behind and requires others to fundamentally change their way of life. This, in turn, can lead to serious discontent among those most affected.

In urban China, for example, tens of millions of employees of the loss-making state-owned enterprises have been let go or forced to take early retirement. In theory, their pensions were guaranteed and a safety net of welfare payments and retraining existed for those no longer employed. In practice, the funds to maintain these support systems were often missing or only a fraction of what was called for in the regulations. Local governments and the state enterprises that were expected to pay for these benefits often did not have the money required. Most of the people let go in this way were in the older age cohorts, and older age cohorts are less likely to be in the vanguard pushing for fundamental political change. It is worth noting, however, that China's leaders in the past stated openly that one of the greatest single obstacles to completing state enterprise reform was the fear of the political consequences of letting so many workers go.

Potentially more disruptive to the political system are three other structural changes that are occurring. Two of these are changes that normally accompany rapid economic growth but have special features peculiar to China that make the process potentially more disruptive. A third is a feature peculiar to China and its one-child policy. These three structural changes by no means exhaust all of the possibilities for social and political tension, but they are among the most important.

One structural change that always accompanies economic growth, rapid or otherwise, is a population shift out of agriculture and the rural areas into industrial and service sector jobs in the cities. As already indicated in our analysis of China's growth prospects, China over the next two decades is likely to experience a massive movement of labor of this kind, the largest rural to urban migration in world history. If China follows the pattern of Japan and South Korea at comparable stages in their economic growth, the share of China's population in agriculture could fall from 50 to 10 percent of the total over the next two decades. Currently (in 2004) there are 757 million people in rural China and 353 million of those are farm workers. A conservative estimate of the movement of farm workers would be a movement out of agriculture mainly to the cities of at least 200 million workers by 2025. If their families go with them, the migration out of the rural areas could reach 400 to 500 million.

But what kind of welcome can these worker migrants and their families expect from the urban population and urban governments? For most of the period of Communist Party rule, China has had a household registration system, the *hukou* system, that assigns people to a residence in either an urban or a rural area. The *hukou* system itself dates back to imperial times, but its use to vigorously restrict rural to urban migration is a modern phenomenon. Under the system as it operated until recently, if a family had a rural *hukou*, it had few rights when moving to the city. Only urban residents were entitled to place their children in the public schools in the cities. Health insurance (when it existed at all) applied only to the regular workers in the enterprises who also had urban registration. Migrants faced the usually impossible task of paying the high costs of urban medical care out of pocket. Furthermore, the massive housing construction that China has undertaken in the urban areas since 1978 has been built, for the most part, for existing urban residents. Migrants were expected to live in factory dormitories or on the construction sites where they worked—anywhere other than in the new housing being constructed by the state and by private developers. China, in effect, has had a two-class system, with a relatively privileged urban population and an underprivileged rural and migrant population. The result has been that many migrants leave their families back in the countryside. Those that do bring their families have to find ways to support themselves and to create their own schools for their children without government support and, not infrequently, with local government harassment.

Dumping another several hundred million people into this system over the coming two decades would appear to be a formula for high tension on an unprecedented scale. The central government in Beijing at least appears to be aware of the problem. Steps have been taken to further weaken the household registration system, replacing it with rules that make it somewhat easier to transfer official residence to an urban location. This, however, has been mainly for people with regular long-term urban employment, a status that does not apply to large numbers of migrants. There has also been a national government decision to allow migrant children to attend urban public schools in part because, according to the national government, the one-child family policy has led to unused capacity in these urban schools. (There has been less effort to deal with the health situation, but that reflects the general disarray in Chinese health care financing and is not peculiar to the migrants.) Perhaps most importantly, there is not as of yet a major effort to provide these urban migrants with minimally adequate housing for their families.

The current shortcomings in the way China is handling rural-to-urban migration could be a source of social and political disaster, with hundreds of millions of young, discontented people struggling to survive in the cities and resorting to crime and demonstrations against perceived abuses. Or this situation could be an opportunity for the Chinese leadership. The recent decision concerning education for migrant children is a good illustration of the latter. If local urban governments really cooperate in this endeavor, families will move to the cities, in part, in order to get a better education for their children. Families trying to push their children up the income and social status ladder are less likely to be involved in antisocial activities. Better education for migrant children will no doubt mean that the number of migrants will increase relative to what otherwise would have been the case, but China will benefit in the long term from having children who have better educational opportunities than they could have received in most rural areas.[36]

Housing for the migrants could also be a major opportunity, not just a high cost burden. As will be discussed later in this essay, China needs to shift demand from its current heavy reliance on the growth of exports to greater reliance on the domestic market. What better place to start than a large-scale housing program that will use domestically produced resources (cement and steel) and lots of labor in general and migrant labor in particular. Furthermore, done well, such a housing program could provide a foundation on which to build a stable urban society that includes most of the population of China. The Peoples Action Party in Singapore gained a large measure of its support from first undertaking a large-scale urban public housing program that housed virtually the entire low-income end of the population, and then proceeded to sell off that housing to those who lived in it at favorable prices and financing terms. Granted that Singapore had to accommodate fewer than 2 million people in this way and China will have to accommodate 500 million or perhaps as many as 25 million a year, the principle is much the same.

Given the way the Chinese governmental system is structured, including the way the various levels of that system are financed, local governments would have to play a major role in this effort, and that is part of the problem. The national government appears to recognize the issues at stake, but it is far less clear that the same can be said of local urban governments. Many of the latter appear to look on migrants as a necessary nuisance and to spend as little money on them as possible.

Another source of potential social tension in China arises directly from the one child per family policy. Because of traditional Chinese values and because of the weakness of the current pension systems, Chinese families, like families elsewhere in many developing countries, have a distinct preference for male children. In the Chinese system, female children marry into their husband's family and in the eyes of many are "lost" to the family into which they were born. With modern methods for determining the sex of children and with the ready availability in China of abortion, many families are opting to abort female fetuses and allow male fetuses to go to term. The practice is illegal in China, but it is extremely difficult to enforce the law. The result in terms of child sex ratios is shown in table 3. Over a twenty-year period, the ratio has gone from fewer males than females to nearly 123 males for every 100 females. If this situation continues for another two decades, in absolute numbers one is talk-

TABLE 3

SEX RATIOS
(number of males per 100 females by age group in 2004)

Aged 20–24	ratio 96.85
Aged 15–19	ratio 107.42
Aged 10–14	ratio 112.43
Aged 5–9	ratio 119.10
Aged 0–4	ratio 122.69

SOURCE: National Bureau of Statistics, 2005, 97.

ing about 25 million excess males in the potentially volatile 15-to-24 age group.

This kind of change for so large a population has no precedent and that makes it virtually impossible to predict the consequences. It is difficult, however, to see this situation as anything other than a major source of potential instability and other forms of antisocial behavior.

The biggest source of potential pressure for political change is from a more conventional source for which there is a great deal of international experience. China today is a nation where a large proportion of the population is still poor and not very well educated relative to the populations of middle and high-income nations. Based on a large sample survey in 2004, only 19.2 percent of China's population over the age of six or a total of 235 million people had either a secondary school or tertiary-level education. In terms of income, the top 40 percent of the urban population or 217 million people had an income per capita of renminbi 8,300 yuan or more or roughly 22,000 yuan per family ($1,000 and $2,700 at the official exchange rate or $4–5,000 and $10,800–13,500 at the PPP exchange rate). In the rural areas, the per capita income of the top 15 percent of the population in 2004, or another 190 million people, averaged over renminbi 5,000 yuan.[37] There is no widely accepted definition of "middle class," but we use the term here to refer to people who are reasonably well educated, are likely to have supervisory or white-collar jobs above the clerical level, or are well-off farmers who can afford to send their children all the way through secondary school. These are people who have significant amounts of discretionary income and have some knowledge of what is happening in the rest of China and even in the rest of the world from television, reading, and even the Internet (there are more than 100 million people with regular access to the Internet in China). It is likely that a substantial majority of the top 40 percent of the income earners in the urban areas and some of the top 15 percent in the rural areas could be considered "middle class" in this sense.

Put differently, these are the people most likely over time to want to have more participation in the major political decisions that affect their lives than they have at present, given the way the Chinese Communist Party and hence the government is organized. They are the kind of people who, if upset enough with the current system, may not go to the streets themselves but will support the activities of students and others who do, as happened in South Korea in 1987 or in China in 1989. Their numbers in China today, however, are still relatively small, perhaps 200 to 300 million adults, about 20 percent of the total population. Over the next twenty years these numbers and their share of the total population will rise rapidly. In income terms, 7 percent per capita growth a year will produce incomes four times the present level. In 2004 there were 4.5 million new entrants into tertiary-level institutions and 8 million new entrants into senior secondary schools. Even though the number of people in the relevant age groups is beginning to decline because of the one-child policy, these enrollment figures will continue to rise rapidly over the coming two decades.

Any precise estimate involves some weakly supported assumptions, but it is likely that at least another 250 million will graduate from senior high school, with over 140 million of those going on to university.[38] Because the percentage of those educated who will die over these coming years is very small, the net increase in the population educated to these levels will be almost the same as this increase in enrollments.[39] Thus, in 2025 the Chinese educated and relatively high-income class or "middle class" will total over 500 million people or nearly 40 percent of the total adult population at that time. A high percentage of those will be under the age of 60. By 2025 most of these people will reside in urban areas. Will these people continue to remain passive politically? Will they remain passive even if China goes through several years of poor economic performance or some other social or political strain? We will have to wait until 2025 to find out the answer to these questions, but from the perspective of 2006, continued passive acceptance of the political status quo does not seem very likely. Will the transition to a new political order be peaceful or violent? Again, even in Asia there is no common pattern that one can point to. The transition in Taiwan was led by then President Chiang Ching-kuo, the transition in South Korea came after large student rioting supported by the middle class, and the transition in Japan came only after defeat in World War II.

Finally, there are international events that could fundamentally alter what, overall, are the favorable prospects for continued Chinese economic growth. This essay is not the place to discuss at length the various foreign policy challenges faced by China. Suffice it to say that a major war in the Straits of Taiwan would fundamentally alter all of the forecasts of future economic growth described above.

The Impact of Future Economic Growth

This essay is primarily about trying to understand the path of Chinese economic growth over the next two decades. One cannot leave the subject, however, without some comments on the implications of this high growth rate for the international economy, the environment, and the world balance of military power.

As discussed briefly above, China's exports in 2005 reached $762 billion and were 6 percent of total world trade. China's foreign exchange reserves by the end of 2006 were projected to pass $1 trillion.[40] The growth rate of exports since the year 2000 has averaged 23 percent per year, and the figure in the most recent years has been higher. If these rates were to continue for the next two decades, China's exports would rise 62-fold and trade as a share of Chinese

GDP would rise to 3 or 4 times China's GDP in 2025. Even in 2005 Chinese exports were 34 percent of Chinese GDP, an extraordinarily high figure for a large country. Large countries in terms of population size tend to have much lower trade ratios than small countries.[41] Japan in the year 2000, by way of comparison, had an export-to-GDP ratio of roughly 11 percent. Chinese total exports in 2025 would be several times the current level of total world exports! There is no question, therefore, that Chinas' export growth rate in percentage terms will come down and will come down sharply sometime within the next few years, or within the next decade at the latest. Even a slower real-growth rate of say 10 percent a year, given the absolute size of the expansion of China's exports at that rate, will put an adjustment strain on countries around the globe, both recipients of those Chinese exports and competitors with China for the same markets. Whether the World Trade Organization could manage those strains is an open question.

China, therefore, clearly must generate most future increases in aggregate demand from domestic sources. China's trade ratio as a share of GDP, already extraordinarily high for such a large country, is likely to level off in the near future. A level or slightly declining trade ratio implies that China's future exports will grow at the same real rate as Chinese GDP or 6 to 8 percent a year. Even that rate will require major adjustments on the part of other trading nations.

One likely change that would both help slow the export growth rate and also slow the rapid increase in China's foreign exchange reserves would be a major revaluation of the Chinese currency. In addition to the need to slow exports for reasons already given, it makes little sense for China to keep on building up foreign exchange reserves. The rate of return on these reserves is very low, given that it is mostly invested in U.S. and other foreign government bonds. These bonds do give China some leverage over U.S. policy in a range of areas, a noneconomic motive for holding them, but the magnitude of that leverage is not as large as it is sometimes portrayed.[42]

Another obvious impact of China's growth on the world economy is on the demand for energy and for petroleum—and natural gas in particular. China's rising demand for oil is widely seen as contributing to high oil prices in 2006, although events in the Middle East often had a bigger impact. The basic nature of China's growing demand is not complicated. China has vast quantities of coal, but coal is creating so many environmental problems that there is a strong desire on the part of the Chinese government to switch out of coal, to a limited degree, and substitute petroleum and natural gas. When the rapid increase in the number of automobiles and other four-wheeled motorized vehicles is added to this situation, China's demand for oil is increasing at a rate faster than that of energy in general; and demand for energy in general is growing at roughly half the rate of GDP if one believes the official statistics. The rate of energy demand growth according to these same official statistics appears to have picked up markedly since the year 2000.[43] The share of petroleum in total energy demand fell from 22.5 percent in 1978 to 17.5 percent in 1995, but since then rose to 24.6 percent in 2000 before falling back to 22.7 percent in 2004.[44]

On the supply side, China's supply of petroleum from domestic sources has grown very slowly—at 1.7 percent a year to 175 million tons (roughly 3.5 million barrels per day)—causing imports to rise rapidly to roughly equal domestic production. Since production in some of China's older fields is declining and new fields are coming online only slowly, most future demand is likely to be met by imports. Forecasts of what this might involve depend critically on the assumptions made to derive those forecasts—notably the assumption about the likely improvement in energy and petroleum use efficiency. Will China match the experience of Japan with highly efficient use of energy or will it match the wasteful practices of the United States? At present China is one of the world's least efficient users of energy when measured as units of energy per unit of GDP. China in 2004 used roughly 0.7 kg of energy per U.S. dollar of GDP as contrasted to Japan, which used only .14 kg per U.S. dollar of GDP, and the United States, which used .24 kg.[45] Much of China's inefficiency reflects the years under central planning, when little if any effort was made to improve energy efficiency and supplies of energy, given China's low level of GDP, were plentiful. Supplies relative to China's GDP are no longer plentiful and the

incentives of a market economy, the severity of the pollution problem, and the low income of much of the Chinese population are all
causing the country to put much more effort into raising energy
efficiency levels. Whether that will bring Chinese energy use to efficiency levels achieved by countries such as Japan remains to be
seen, but the efficiency level is bound to rise markedly. If as a result
of these efficiency measures petroleum-use growth fell a little below
GDP growth over the next two decades, China by 2025 would
probably be importing oil at a rate of roughly 17 million barrels
per day.[46] The U.S. Energy Department estimates, in contrast, that
China in 2025 will be importing 10.9 million barrels per day, a relatively conservative estimate.[47] At the extreme upper end is environmental analyst Lester Brown's estimate for Chinese domestic oil
consumption of 99 million barrels per day in 2031 if present
Chinese policies continue unchanged.[48]

If China does require oil imports of 11 to 17 million barrels a day,
the country will probably have the foreign exchange to pay for it. At
$70 per barrel, the higher figure would cost China $434 billion per
year in 2025, when China's total exports (in today's prices) would be
around $3 trillion. But would prices in real terms stay at $70 with
Chinese imports of this magnitude? It would all depend on a com-
bination of world efforts to cut back on the demand for petroleum-
products together with the supply response of petroleum-producing
nations. That is a subject for another essay.

High energy consumption along with industrial development in
general, of course, also has major implications for the environment.
Recent visitors to Chinese cities regularly comment on the poor air
quality. Many rivers are filled with chemical wastes from nearby factories. There are now many environmental laws on the books, and
China's environmental protection authorities have become increasingly vigorous over time in the difficult task of trying to enforce these
laws. But is the environmental situation in China serious enough to
alter our forecast of long-term growth?

Clearly China has been forced to face up to the environmental
consequences of rapid economic growth at a much lower per capita
income than was the case in the United States, Europe, or Japan. But

FIGURE 1

AIR POLLUTION IN CHINA AND ITS NEIGHBORS

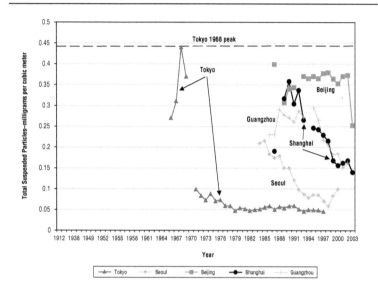

SOURCE: Thomas G. Rawski, "Urban Air Quality in China: Historical and Comparative Perspectives" (working paper, International Center for the Study of East Asian Development, Kitakyushu, Japan, 2006).

is the problem significantly worse in China than in these earlier advanced countries and is the cost of dealing with the problem large enough to affect economic growth? There are various ways of measuring the level of pollutants in Chinese air and water. Here in figure 1 we only present the data for the total number of particulates in the air in China and compare it with similar measures for Tokyo and Seoul from earlier periods. The figure is from a recent study by economics professor Thomas Rawski.[49] Other tables in that study compare some of China's most polluted cities with Pittsburgh. The main point of this figure is to show that China's level of air pollution, bad as it is, is not significantly different from the situation in Tokyo in 1968, Pittsburgh in 1920, or Seoul in the early 1980s. Furthermore, as the figure makes clear, the level of pollution in China's major cities, while still very high, is coming down despite continued rapid economic development. Efforts to reduce pollution are having an effect.

How expensive is this ongoing effort to control pollution? By the mid-1990s, the Dutch Sinologist Eduard Vermeer estimates that China was spending 1.4 percent of GDP on the prevention and treatment of pollution.[50] That is a large figure in absolute terms but it clearly is not going to be a major influence slowing overall Chinese GDP growth. At a 4:1 incremental capital-output ratio, roughly China's current level, this expenditure on pollution treatment and control would reduce growth by 0.35 percent per year. If a reduction in pollution levels increased overall health and efficiency in the cities, the impact on growth would be that much less.

While China appears quite capable of eventually reducing air and water pollution emanating from its factories at an acceptable cost, reducing particulates and SO_2 will not slow China's impact on CO_2 emissions resulting from the consumption of hydrocarbons. China's rapidly increasing contribution to global warming, therefore, will continue. It will be some time before China's impact on global climate change is comparable to that of the United States, but China's impact is significant today and will grow along with the projected rise in China's use of coal and petroleum. If global warming is to be slowed and eventually reversed, clearly China is going to have to play a major role in reducing its consumption of hydrocarbons per unit of GDP. Put differently, given that China under any realistic assumptions will continue to experience steadily rising emissions of CO_2 even if it makes significant strides toward greater efficiency in energy use, the rest of the world, and especially the United States, will have to make far greater efforts than at present if global warming is to be contained. How China, the United States, and the rest of the world should go about achieving these reductions is a subject for another essay.

Finally, a few words are in order about the impact of continued Chinese growth on the size of the Chinese military budget. For many years after the start of the reform period, China held down its military expenditures. In real terms there was scarcely any increase in expenditure at all. As a result, Chinese military expenditures as a share of GDP actually declined significantly. Beginning in 1997, however, Chinese military expenditures began to grow at a pace similar to the rapid growth of GDP. Estimates of the change in military expenditures in real terms are presented in table 4 on the following page. Real expenditures by 2003 nearly doubled the level of 1997, and the rate of growth has continued since. The question of why China began expanding defense expenditures in 1997 is not known, but there are several plausible explanations. The level of Chinese military technology prior to 1997 was stuck in an earlier era and it probably made little sense for China to invest more in the production of obsolete fighter aircraft, tanks, or infantry weapons. There is also the possibility that China was influenced by the first U.S. attack on Iraq in 1991 following Iraq's invasion of Kuwait. In that brief war, American high-tech weapons obliterated a Soviet-weapons–equipped Iraqi military in a matter of a few weeks. Given that China's military was also equipped with Soviet-type weapons, many of them less advanced than those of Iraq, it is reasonable to assume that China's military planners saw a need to fundamentally rethink and upgrade their military technology and equipment.[51] Finally, once military modernization was underway in the 1990s and was increasing at roughly the same rate as GDP, politics, notably the need of the civilians in charge of the government to keep the military content, ensured that military expenditures would continue to grow regardless of external threat projections or the lack thereof.[52]

Whatever the motives for the change in growth of military expenditures in the 1990s, therefore, there is every reason to think that China will continue to expand its military expenditures in the years to come. Barring a security crisis affecting China or a fundamental change in the strategic challenge facing China, a plausible assumption is that continued rapid GDP growth will enable China to expand military expenditures at a rate similar to the growth rate of GDP. China's almost certain long-term goal is to move from being able to defend the Chinese homeland to being able to reach military parity with the United States. That goal depends as much on the progress of Chinese military technology as it does on the country's

TABLE 4

CHINESE OFFICIAL AND ESTIMATED DEFENSE EXPENDITURES

Year	Official Defense Budget (billion yuan, current prices)	Official Defense Budget (as a Share of GDP)	Estimated Defense Budget (official budget x 2; billion yuan, current prices)	"Real" National Defense Expenditures (billion yuan, 2003 prices)
1978	16.78	0.046	33.56	Na
1980	19.38	0.043	38.76	Na
1985	19.15	0.021	38.30	113.7
1990	29.03	0.016	58.06	97.2
1991	33.03	0.015	66.06	102.8
1992	37.79	0.014	75.58	104.6
1993	42.58	0.012	85.16	95.6
1994	55.07	0.012	110.14	96.0
1995	63.67	0.011	127.34	95.5
1996	72.01	0.011	144.02	100.3
1997	81.26	0.011	162.52	109.1
1998	93.47	0.012	186.94	120.0
1999	107.64	0.013	215.28	133.1
2000	120.75	0.013	241.50	140.0
2001	144.20	0.015	288.40	157.9
2002	170.78	0.016	341.56	180.0
2003	190.79	0.016	381.58	190.8

SOURCE AND METHODOLOGY: Perkins, 2005, 380. The figure for real expenditures was obtained by first doubling the size of the officially reported military budget because of the widespread view that the official budget understates total expenditures by at least that much (Shambaugh, 2002). These figures are divided into wages of military personnel and military equipment and the former is deflated by a state sector wage index and the latter by a price index for industrial products (the ex-factory price index).

NOTE: Na = data not available for price deflation.

willingness to spend money on defense, but over time the size of the Chinese defense budget could match that of the United States. Parity with the United States in dollars spent, however, will not be reached within the two-decade time frame with which this discussion is concerned.[53] China long before that, however, will almost certainly have the second largest defense budget in the world, and it is not far away from that target today. At present, depending on just what exchange rate one uses, China is already in a group of nations (France, Germany, Japan, and Russia) that are next after the United States in total military expenditures, with the United States' expenditures being far ahead of all four combined.

Implications for United States Policy

This essay is not primarily about United States foreign policy, but there are some clear implications for the United States if the Chinese economy continues its rapid growth. China's rapid growth of exports and imports is already receiving the attention of American politicians, policymakers, and the general public. Even if this export growth slows markedly down to the rate of growth of GDP as suggested above, China will be on the regular agenda of American trade negotiators for decades to come. This will be the case even though China today has a trade and foreign investment regime that is much more open than were those of South Korea, Taiwan, or Japan at a comparable stage of development. Given the absence in China of a legal system capable of rigorously enforcing intellectual property rights, for example, there will be ongoing demands from American producers of intellectual property followed by efforts by the Chinese to meet those demands at least partway. These negotiations may involve tension between the two parties, but ultimately protection of property rights is in the interest of both; it is just that it is more in the interest of the United States at this stage of its development than it is of China at its stage of development.

China's current account surplus situation, however, may or may not be an ongoing problem. If China does what it probably should do for its own sake and revalues its currency in a major way, that current account surplus would shrink and possibly disappear. No Chinese revaluation, however, will solve the U.S. current account deficit, and thus the bilateral trade deficit between China and the United States is likely to continue.[54] The U.S. deficit is a product of Americans' spending more for goods and services that the rest of the world produces than they are earning on sales of goods and services to that world. No plausible amount of Chinese trade liberalization or revaluation will solve that problem. The solution lies mainly in America.

The impact of China on the world energy market and the market for other minerals is not really an item for negotiation. It is simply a fact to which the rest of the world will have to adjust. Energy security does have some implications for China's military security, notably the protection of the sea lanes that carry petroleum destined for China. For the most part, however, these are the same sea lanes that bring oil to Japan and South Korea, so the interests of the major parties in Northeast Asia should be aligned most of the time.[55] Outside of these kinds of security issues, rising mineral prices should generate all of the supply response that is feasible without any assistance from government policy of any of the major producers and consumers of energy.

The environmental situation does require government action, particularly action by the U.S. government. China's air and water pollution problems are a Chinese problem and will be dealt with by China, no doubt with the help of environmentally supportive technology developed in part by companies in the United States and elsewhere. China's growing CO_2 emissions, however, require action of governments around the world to rein in the worldwide growth of CO_2. There is no acceptable way to slow the growth of China's CO_2 emissions below a level comparable to that of the more energy-efficient users around the world. It in fact will take a major effort by China to reach that slower level of growth. The country with the widest economic and technological discretion to do something about worldwide CO_2 growth is clearly the United States, either as part of an international agreement or unilaterally. Whether the U.S. government has the political will to take advantage of this situation, however, remains to be seen.

The growth of China's military expenditures is also a fact that cannot be radically altered by the policies of the United States or by other outside powers short of war. The one exception to this statement is in the area of military use technology, where the United States and other nations already impose restrictions. Clearly the rise of Chinese military power is gradually going to change the balance of military power in Asia. What is far less clear is whether this changing balance of power will alter significantly any of the current relationships between China and its neighbors. For the most part, the answer is probably that changes in these relationships will be modest. Border disputes do exist between China and India, between China and Japan over islands lying between the two countries, and between China and other claimants to islands in the South China Sea, but it is hard to see how a rational Chinese government would try to resolve these disputes by force alone. China probably could seize many of the disputed areas that it does not now control, but the main effect would be to create a ring of hostile nations around its borders no doubt backed by U.S. power.

The one big exception to the above relatively benign view of Chinese power is Taiwan and the balance of power between China and Taiwan's implicit protector, the United States. If the Chinese military budget increases fourfold over the coming two decades and its military technology improves rapidly along with these expenditures, there will be a shift in the balance of power in the Straits of Taiwan. The potential costs to U.S. support for Taiwan will go up, with implications for U.S. policy that are difficult to predict and are way beyond the scope of this essay. We simply note here that the shift is real and the implications are profound for all of the parties involved.

Finally, there is the basic question of whether or not continued rapid growth in China is itself in America's interests. The unequivocal answer of this writer is yes. The alternatives are all much worse. A rapidly growing China integrated into the world economic system and the world political system is a China with a strong vested interest in stability. It does not follow that China will buy stability at all costs in order to continue rapid economic growth, but it will do so in most circumstances. Rapid economic growth is also the best hope, probably the only real hope, for the kind of domestic political changes in China that will build a foundation for long-term stability in China both domestically and internationally. Will these changes occur in a reasonable time frame? The obvious answer is we don't know—they may occur or they may not, but what is the alternative if one wants to achieve political reform? This statement about domestic political change fostering stability may seem like a contradiction to the earlier discussion of how the rapid rise of a large middle class could create political instability in China. Instability in the short run, caused by the population demanding full participation in the political process, may in fact be a cost that has to be paid to reach the kind of participation and pluralism in the political system that will fortify stability over the long run.

Could this growth all go wrong and lead to domestic crises that bring nationalistic politicians to the fore, politicians willing to use the military to back up claims to "lost" Chinese territory? The obvious answer is that this could happen, but that it is far more likely to happen if China is careening from one economic crisis to another. If growth slows or even stops altogether, job growth will disappear, incomes of those with jobs will stagnate or fall, and discontent will spread rapidly. The leaders of the government presiding over this end to growth will no doubt lose their jobs, and they will be replaced. China could have a rebellious population and a leadership playing the nationalist card, all in a country with a large nuclear arsenal and the missiles to deliver them. The risks of an increasingly rich and powerful China are to be preferred.

Notes

1. There is some debate over whether this officially estimated growth rate overstates China's true rate of GDP growth. Notably, however, when China's National Bureau of Statistics in 2005 adjusted their GDP estimates to better take into account the growth in the services sector, the result was a small increase in the growth rate. That said, there are certainly reasons for thinking that GDP growth in years such as 1997–1999 may have been overstated (see Thomas Rawski, 2001), but there is also scholarly work supporting the view that GDP growth may have been understated (Kojima, 2002, and Klein et al., 2005). Whatever the precise figure, there is no question that China's GDP growth rate has been very rapid in comparison to that of most other countries.

2. Maddison, 1995, 202–203.

3. Maddison, 1995, 194–195.

4. This statement is based on World Bank data and excludes the countries that have been formed out of the breakup of Yugoslavia. Estimates of GDP in U.S. dollars or in purchasing power parity for former centrally planned economies are fraught with methodological problems. Thus the statement in the text here should be taken as a general indicator of performance in these countries. Slightly different methodologies would give somewhat different results, but the basic fact of an economic decline in much of the region is not in doubt.

5. This figure is for 1978. The figure in the statistical yearbook is given in per capita terms and I have multiplied the number by 3. State Statistical Bureau, 1982, 429.

6. National Bureau of Statistics, 2005, 333.

7. A Chinese government official with whom I was working in the early 1980s had spent the whole day trying to get through from Beijing to Shanghai to arrange our appointments without success. According to him, the capacity of the phone system for all of China was roughly equal to that of the city of Hong Kong alone.

8. In 1960 the total number of vehicles on Japanese roads (including trucks and buses) was only 1.35 million but that figure rose rapidly in

subsequent years to reach 25 million vehicles in 1973 (Japan Automobile Manufacturers Association web page, 2006).

9. Based on personal observation.

10. Answers.com, "Lufthansa," www.answers.com/Lufthansa.

11. Wikipedia, "American Airlines," http://en.wikipedia.org/American_airlines.

12. Based on personal observation.

13. This figure was obtained by multiplying the expenditure level in 1980 in current prices by the retail price index (the rural consumer price index does not go back to 1980 but the retail price index and consumer price index tend to track each other fairly closely).

14. This ratio was obtained from data in World Bank, 2003, 234. Until the Chinese government officially joins the UN system for calculating purchasing power parity exchange rates, however, any estimate such as the one used here is subject to a larger than normal margin for error.

15. Chen and Ravallion, 2004.

16. These 2004 data are derived from the census of the year 2000 and sample surveys conducted by the National Bureau of Statistics for subsequent years (National Bureau of Statistics, 2005, 92–93, 115–118). There are significant problems with these data, particularly the employment data, but the basic trend that they reflect is not in doubt.

17. These remarks are based in part on personal observation during trips to China in 1974 and 1975 and in part on numerous reports verbally and in writing from numerous other visitors to China.

18. An all-encompassing ideology to which adherence was demanded and police terror to back it up were the first two components of the definition of totalitarianism. The other four components of the Friedrich-Brzezinski definition were a "single mass party hierarchically organized and closely interwoven with the state bureaucracy and typically led by one man, monopolistic control of the armed forces, monopoly of the effective means of communication, and central control and direction of the economy." (Plueger, 2006). China also met these other four criteria for being a totalitarian system.

19. *New York Times* columnist Nicholas Kristof experimented during a recent visit to China with what could be found easily on the Internet when in China; he was able to reach some blocked sites and was able to tell quite easily in some cases what passages or terms were being blocked (Kristof, 2005).

20. Transparency International, 2005.

21. World Bank, 2006, 92.

22. These trends are discussed in more depth in Perkins and Rawski, 2006.

23. Because of the encroachment of urban and industrial development, China's arable land has been declining and has fallen from 130 million hectares in the late 1990s (Fu Jing, 2006, 1).

24. Perkins and Rawski, 2006.

25. To be more precise, migrants into the urban workforce will take over many existing as well as new unskilled jobs, freeing up the better educated urbanites to fill the increases in higher skilled jobs.

26. Between 1978 and 1984 the primary sector value-added rose at an annual rate of 7.3 percent per year. From the end of 1984 through 2004 that rate was 3.8 percent per year. Between 1957 and 1978 the gross value of agricultural output grew at only 2.3 percent per year (Rural Society and Economy Investigation Team of the National Bureau of Statistics, 2000, 33) as contrasted to a gross value output rate of increase from 1984 to 2004 of 5.7 percent per year. The gross value growth rate figures particularly for the most recent years are higher than the value-added data largely because agriculture was making increasing use of purchased inputs in the more recent years. Greater efficiency in the use of inputs that may also have been occurring would have brought the value-added growth rates closer to those for gross value of output. A major reason why agricultural growth in the post-1984 period was higher than in the pre-1978 period was that farmers were freer to plant higher valued crops rather than having to concentrate mainly on grain crops.

27. Yusuf, Nabeshima, and Perkins, 2006, 80.

28. From the beginning there was always considerable regional variation in the ownership classification of TVEs. In Guangdong Province, outright private ownership was acceptable early on, whereas in major TVE centers such as Wuxi in Jiangsu Province, outright private ownership in the 1980s was generally not acceptable. William A. Byrd and Qingsong Lin, *China's Rural Industry: Structure, Development, and Reform* (New York: Oxford University Press, 1990).

29. For a discussion of the origins of the dual price system see Hua, Zhang, and Luo, 1993, 119–131.

30. One estimate based on statistics from the Ministry of Land and Resources reported in the Chinese press is that one in two construction projects between October 2004 and May 2005 were built on land acquired illegally. (Fu Jing, 2006).

31. Prior to the reform period the banks lent mainly to state enterprises as well (and to rural communes) because state enterprises plus some collectives were all there were. But prior to the 1980s, loans were only for working capital while investment capital was supplied directly from the government budget. With the reforms, the system of having most industrial investment

handled through the budget was abandoned and replaced with loans for investment from the commercial banks to the enterprises.

32. For an in-depth discussion of the origins of the nonperforming assets of the banking system, see Lardy, 1998.

33. This figure was given by the then-governor of the central bank, Dai Xianglong. The transfer of a substantial portion of these bad loans to separate asset management companies reduced the nonperforming assets still in the banks to 25 percent of total assets. The criteria used in arriving at these percentages, however, are seen by many as understating the total (Lardy, 2001).

34. In South Korea, particularly by the 1990s, industrial policy became increasingly politicized and corrupt, and that was one of several reasons why South Korea began to try to replace its active industrial policy with a more market-oriented system, but this proved difficult to do in practice.

35. The arguments in these paragraphs are developed at greater length in Perkins, 2004.

36. China's leadership is also trying to put more resources into rural schools, but rural schools in most developing countries suffer from a handicap that is very difficult to overcome. It is extremely difficult to get well-trained teachers to go to the rural areas to teach. Even those from the rural areas that go on to get sufficient education to be comparable to urban teachers usually do so in order to get out of the rural areas, not to return to them to teach.

37. These data are all from or derived from National Bureau of Statistics, 2005, and are mainly based on rural and urban household surveys taken annually.

38. This assumes that enrollments and graduates of secondary schools will average over 12 million per year (the current enrollment level in 2004 was 8 million) and that more than 7 million a year will go on to university (the current enrollment level in 2004 was 4.5 million). Because the size of the relevant age cohorts is declining due to the one-child policy, the percentage of the relevant age cohorts going on to upper secondary and tertiary education will be higher than the absolute rise in numbers of enrollments and graduates.

39. Only 1.7 percent of the total population in 1964 (census data) or 12 million people had either a secondary level or some tertiary level of education and most of that education occurred after 1949. Presumably most of the people dying over the next twenty years will be those born before 1949 (who will be aged 76 or older) and those born in the 1950s, who will range in age from 65 to 75 in 2025. The number of graduates of tertiary schools in the 1950s was 480 thousand and the number of graduates of senior

secondary schools was 1.2 million (National Bureau of Statistics, *Zhongguo tongji nianjian*, 1989, 799–800). To that should be added several tens of thousands of tertiary-level students from before 1950 and an unknown but small number of secondary school graduates who would still be alive in 2005. The total number of university graduates in China in the period 1913–1947 was 210 thousand and 174 thousand were estimated to be still alive in 1960 (Orleans, 1961, 126).

40. David Barboza, "China's Surge Raises Fears of Runaway Economy," *New York Times*, July 19, 2006.

41. The relationship between country size measured in terms of population and the ratio of trade to GDP was first noted by Simon Kuznets.

42. The Chinese government, for example, has already decided to diversify its foreign exchange holdings and it could in the future decide to get out of U.S. Treasury bonds altogether. But these bonds would still be sold to someone, albeit at a somewhat higher rate of interest. How high the interest rate rise would have to be would be a function not just of the market for U.S. government bonds but of the worldwide market for instruments of this kind and of bonds in general. The rise would thus be much smaller than would be the case if the U.S. Treasury bond market operated in isolation from other capital markets.

43. Chinese energy consumption and production figures are a bit treacherous, in part because reporting from small coal mines is often inaccurate. Thus, for example, the government repeatedly orders the closing of many of these mines but local authorities and mine owners regularly keep the mines open. Eventually they stop reporting production in those mines. Total energy demand grew according to official figures between 1978 and 2004 at an average annual rate of 4.9 percent as compared to GDP growth at a 9.1 percent rate. But from the end of 2000 through 2004, energy consumption grew at 10.9 percent.

44. These percentages should be used with caution. Some of the fluctuation in the percentage oil contributes to energy demand may only reflect the inaccuracies in the estimates of coal consumption. National Bureau of Statistics, 2005, 255.

45. These calculations were made by the author. China reports its consumption of energy in terms of a "standard coal equivalent," whereas Japan and others report data in terms of standard crude oil equivalent. The Chinese data were taken from the National Bureau of Statistics, 2005, and GDP was converted into U.S. dollars at 8.1 yuan = $1.00. The Japanese and U.S. energy consumption data came from Japan External Trade Organization, 2002, 75.

46. This assumes that oil demand grows at 6 percent per year to reach 22 million barrels per day in 2025, with 5 million barrels per day supplied from domestic sources.

47. This estimate assumes total Chinese demand of 14.2 million barrels per day and domestic production of 3.3 million barrels per day.

48. Lester Brown's point is that such a level of imports would be impossible given the size of the world oil market among other reasons (AFP, 2006).

49. Thomas Rawski, 2006, figure 2.

50. Vermeer, 1998, 956.

51. I am indebted for this insight to a participant in the discussion following this lecture at the American Enterprise Institute.

52. Shambaugh, 2005, 82–85.

53. Any precise discussion of when China might achieve parity involves assumptions about the U.S. military budget that are outside the frame of reference of this essay. Parity in terms of actual military capacity requires a judgment about the level of U.S. and Chinese military technology at some future date, a judgment that is well beyond the capacity of the author of this essay.

54. Over time it is possible that the bilateral China-U.S. current account deficit will shift in part to being a deficit with countries other than China, just as what was once a U.S.–Japan, Korea, Taiwan deficit turned into a U.S.-China deficit when those other East Asian countries shifted much of their labor-intensive manufacturing and assembly facilities into China. These other countries still produced much of the value-added in the goods going to the U.S. market but the final production and assembly were in China, so these were defined as "Chinese goods."

55. The most obvious exception to this statement would be if there were a war in the Taiwan Straits and the United States or some other power opted to try to embargo oil going to China, but scenarios of this sort are well beyond the scope of this paper.

References

AFP. "Lester Brown: China growth unsustainable on all counts, must change," May 26, 2006.

Barboza, David. 2006. "China's Surge Raises Fears of Runaway Economy." *New York Times*, July 19.

Byrd, William and Lin Qingsong, eds. *China's Rural Industry: Structure, Development, and Reform.* New York: Oxford University Press, 1990.

Chen, Shaohua and Ravallion, Martin. "How have the world's poorest fared since the 1980s?" Development Research Group. World Bank, 2004.

Fu Jing. "Curbs placed on land use rights, farmers to be better compensated." *The China Daily*, July 28, 2006, p.1

Hua, Sheng, Zhang Xuejun, and Luo Xiaopeng, *China: From Revolution to Reform.* London: MacMillan, 1993.

Japan Automobile Manufacturers Association. http://www.jama.org.2006.

Japan External Trade Organization. *Nippon 2002: Business Facts and Figures.* Tokyo: JETRO, 2002.

Klein, L. R., Huiqing Gao, and Liping Tao in "Estimation of China's Inflation Rate" (draft paper 2005).

Kojima, Reiitsu. "On the Reliability of China's Economic Statistics with Special Reference to GDP." *The Journal of Econometric Study of Northeast Asia* 4, no. 1 (2002): 15–30.

Kristof, Nicholas. 2006. "In China it is ******* vs. Netizens." *New York Times*, June 20.

Lardy, Nicholas. *China's Unfinished Economic Revolution.* Washington: Brookings, 1998.

———. "China's Worsening Debts." *The Financial Times*, June 22, 2001.

Maddison, Angus. *Monitoring the World Economy 1820–1992.* Paris: OECD Development Centre, 1995.

National Bureau of Statistics. *Zhongguo tongji nianjian, 1989.* Beijing: China Statistics Press, 1989.

———. *China Statistical Yearbook, 2005.* Beijing: China Statistics Press, 2005.

Orleans, Leo. *Professional Manpower and Education in Communist China.* Washington: National Science Foundation, 1961.

Perkins, Dwight H. "China's Economic Growth: Implications for the Defense Budget," in Ashley J. Tellis and Michael Wills, eds., *Strategic Asia 2005–06: Military Modernization in an Era of Uncertainty.* Seattle: National Bureau of Asian Research, 2005.

—————. "Corporate Governance, Industrial Policy, and the Rule of Law," in Shahid Yusuf, M. Anjum Altaf, and Kaoru Nabeshima, eds., *Global Change and East Asian Policy Initiatives.* Washington: World Bank and Oxford University Press, 2004, 293–336.

Perkins, Dwight H. and Thomas G. Rawski. "Forecasting China's Economic Growth over the Next Two Decades." 2006 draft, forthcoming in a volume edited by Loren Brandt and Thomas Rawski.

Plueger, Gilbert. *Totalitarianism.* http://www.history-ontheweb.co.uk. (2006)

Rawski, Thomas. "What's Happening to China's GDP Statistics?" *China Economic Review* (December 2001): 347–54.

—————. "Urban Air Quality in China: Historical and Comparative Perspectives," unpublished draft, June 25, 2006.

Rural Society and Economy Investigation Team of the National Bureau of Statistics. *Xin Zhongguo wushinian nongye tongji culiao* [Fifty years of agricultural statistical materials of New China]. Beijing: China Statistics Press, 2000.

Shambaugh, David. "Calculating China's Military Expenditure." Report prepared for the Council on Foreign Relations, Task Force on Chinese Military Power, June 25, 2002.

—————. "China's Military Modernization: Making Steady and Surprising Progress," in Ashley J. Tellis and Michael Wills, eds., *Strategic Asia 2005–06: Military Modernization in an Era of Uncertainty.* Seattle: National Bureau of Asian Research, 2005.

State Statistical Bureau. *Statistical Yearbook of China, 1981.* Hong Kong: Economic Information and Agency, 1982.

Transparency International. *Transparency International Corruption Perceptions Index, 2005.* http://www.transparency.org.

Vermeer, Eduard. "Industrial Pollution in China and Remedial Policies." *The China Quarterly,* no. 156 Special Issue: China's Environment (December 1998): 952–985.

World Bank. *Doing Business in China in 2006: Creating Jobs.* Washington: World Bank, 2006.

—————. *Sustainable Development in a Dynamic World/World Development Report 2003.* New York: Oxford University Press, 2003.

Yusuf, Shahid, Kaoru Nabeshima, and Dwight H. Perkins. *Under New Ownership: Privatizing China's State-Owned Enterprises.* Stanford: Stanford University Press, 2006.

About the Author

Dwight H. Perkins is the Harold Hitchings Burbank Professor of Political Economy at Harvard University, whose faculty he joined in 1963. His previous positions at Harvard include associate director of the East Asian (now Fairbank) Research Center; chairman of the Department of Economics; and director of the Harvard Institute for International Development. Mr. Perkins has authored or edited twelve books and over a hundred articles on economic history and economic development, with special emphasis on the economies of China, Korea, Vietnam, and the other nations of East and Southeast Asia. He has served as an advisor or consultant on economic policy and reform to the governments of Korea, China, Malaysia, Vietnam, Indonesia, and Papua New Guinea. He has also been a long-term consultant to the World Bank, the Ford Foundation, various private corporations, and governmental agencies, including the U.S. Senate Permanent Subcommittee on Investigations. He has been a visiting professor or scholar at Hitotsubashi University in Tokyo, the University of Washington, and Fudan University in Shanghai.